OUR LIVING PLANET

Weather

BLACKBIRCH®
PRESS

THOMSON
GALE

San Diego • Detroit • New York • San Francisco • Cleveland
New Haven, Conn. • Waterville, Maine • London • Munich

THOMSON
───────*───────
GALE

For more information, contact
The Gale Group, Inc.
27500 Drake Rd.
Farmington Hills, MI 48331-3535
Or you can visit our Internet site at http://www.gale.com

Adapted by A S Publishing from
El Tiempo © Parramon Ediciones S.A. 1996

Text: Miquel Àngel Gilbert
Illustrations: Miquel Ferrón, Txema Retama
Design: Beatriz Seoane

Every effort has been made to trace the owners of copyrighted material.

LIBRARY OF CONGRESS CATALOGING-IN-PUBLICATION DATA

Gilbert, Miquel Àngel.
  Weather / by Miquel Àngel Gilbert.
    v. cm. — (Living planet series)
Includes index.
Contents: Introduction: The power of the sun — The protecting atmosphere — Hot and cold — Air pressure — What a wind! — Clouds — Rain, snow and hail — Stormy weather — Future weather.
  ISBN 1-56711-683-3 (hbk. : alk. paper)
  1. Weather—Juvenile literature. 2. Climatology—Juvenile literature. [1. Weather. 2. Meteorology.] I. Title. II. Series.
  QC981.3 .G55 2003
  551.6—dc21   2002009531

Printed in Spain
10 9 8 7 6 5 4 3 2 1

CONTENTS

THE POWER OF THE SUN

The condition of the atmosphere—cold or warm, wet or dry, windy or calm—is called the weather. Although the weather can change from day to day, it does so according to a pattern that is repeated from season to season and from year to year. The pattern of weather in a particular region is known as its climate. Both weather and climate affect our lives in many ways.

Weather is the condition of the atmosphere at one place at one time. Climate is the pattern of weather over a long period in a particular region.

What causes weather? Why does it vary from region to region? Why does it vary from day to day within the same region? The answer to all these questions is the sun. The sun heats the earth. Its rays travel through the atmosphere—the air around us—and heat the ground. The heated ground warms the air. Because the earth is a sphere, the sun does not heat the earth evenly. The sun is almost directly overhead at the equator. Its rays hit the ground straight on, so the heat is intense. Farther away from the equator, the sun is lower in the sky. Because its rays hit the earth at an angle and are spread over a greater area, the heat is less strong. This is why it is always cold at the poles and warm in the tropics, the regions north and south of the equator. In the tropics, plants grow thick and fast; at the poles, it is so icy that nothing will grow.

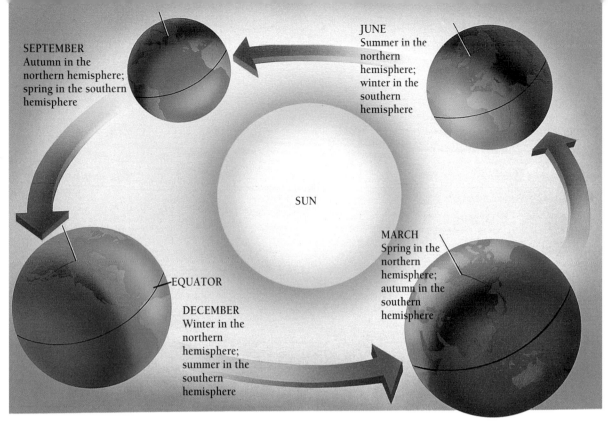

SEPTEMBER
Autumn in the northern hemisphere; spring in the southern hemisphere

JUNE
Summer in the northern hemisphere; winter in the southern hemisphere

SUN

EQUATOR

MARCH
Spring in the northern hemisphere; autumn in the southern hemisphere

DECEMBER
Winter in the northern hemisphere; summer in the southern hemisphere

The earth spins like a top in space. It makes one complete turn every twenty-four hours. Night follows day as it turns. As it spins on its axis, the earth also travels around the sun. The earth takes a year to make each circuit. But the earth does not spin upright; its axis is tilted at an angle of 23 1/2°. This tilt points one side of the orbiting earth toward the sun and then the other. Although the heat and light given out by the sun is always the same, the parts of the earth that lean toward the sun receive more light and heat than the parts tilted away from it. These variations cause the seasons.

In regions that lean toward the sun, it is summer. In regions tilted away from the sun, it is winter. In between these seasons are spring or autumn. The exceptions are at the poles and at the equator. In these regions, the temperature is almost constant all year long: very low at the poles and very high near the equator. At the poles themselves, the sun stays below the horizon for half the year. During the other half, it hangs low in the sky but never sets.

The regions in between have four distinct seasons. Their climate is temperate. A temperate climate is good for growing crops because it is not too hot, cold, wet, or dry.

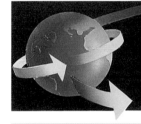

The rhythm of the seasons is caused by the tilt of the earth as it spins from the vertical to its path around the sun.

SUMMER

WINTER

SPRING

AUTUMN

THE PROTECTING ATMOSPHERE

The atmosphere is a layer of air that surrounds the earth. Air is a mixture of transparent gases. Nitrogen accounts for 78 percent and oxygen 21 percent. The remaining 1 percent consists of argon, carbon dioxide, and minute traces of other gases. Water vapor is also present in the air, but the amounts can vary. In desert regions, it is less than 1 percent of the air, while in the tropics, it may account for more than 4 percent.

The atmosphere is vital to life. Without oxygen, human beings could not

The atmosphere shields the earth from harmful rays of the sun and helps to keep it warm.

EXOSPHERE (310 miles [500 km]–space)

THERMOSPHERE (49.6–310 miles [80–500 m])

MESOSPHERE (31–49.6 miles [50–80 km])

OZONE LAYER

STRATOSPHERE (6.2–31 miles [10–50km])

TROPOSPHERE (up to 6.2–9.9 miles 0–16km])

EARTH'S SURFACE

breathe, and without carbon dioxide, plants could not grow. The atmosphere not only provides these essentials but protects us as well. It acts as both a shield and a blanket, so that the earth does not overheat during the day or lose too much heat at night.

The atmosphere reaches as high as 310 miles (500 km) above the earth and consists of five layers. The lowest, the troposphere, is next to the earth. It is where the clouds,

winds, and other weather features are found. Above it is the stratosphere, where supersonic aircraft fly. The ozone layer at the upper edge of the stratosphere stretches like a thin skin around it and merges into the mesosphere.

In all these layers, the temperature decreases with height. In the mesosphere, the temperature falls to minus -248°F (-120°C). A dramatic change occurs in

the next layer, the thermosphere, for here the temperature rises with height and can exceed 3632°F (2000°C). Shooting stars and polar auroras are found in this layer. It is also where the space shuttle flies. Beyond this layer is the exosphere, which is even hotter than the thermosphere. This layer is where the earth's atmosphere gradually merges into space. Some satellites orbit the earth in this region.

The troposphere, the lowest layer of the atmosphere, is the one that supports all human and animal life. It is only about 9.9 miles (16 km) deep at most, but it contains three-quarters of the gases of the atmosphere and almost all of its humidity. Its temperature decreases by about 10.8°F (6°C) for each 3,281 feet (1,000 m) of height. Its lowest level contains dust particles and salt crystals. The dust in the atmosphere is what makes sunsets appear red.

The air in the troposphere acts as a thermostat to maintain temperatures over the earth. It moderates the heat from the sun so that it does not escape too rapidly into space. The heat and water in the troposphere combine to give us our weather.

The sun emits not only the infrared heat rays that warm us but also ultraviolet (UV) rays. These rays tan and burn the skin and can cause cancer. The earth is shielded from over 95 percent of UV rays by a layer of ozone gas in the upper stratosphere. Ozone (O_3) is a form of oxygen (O_2) that has three, rather than two, oxygen atoms. Chemicals called chlorofluorocarbons (CFCs), which are used in refrigerants and aerosol sprays, react with the ozone molecules and break them down into oxygen molecules. Without the ozone, too many damaging ultraviolet rays can reach the earth.

The bottom layer of the atmosphere, the troposphere, is where the weather takes place.

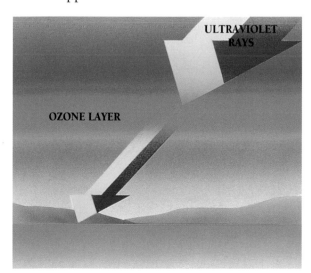

ULTRAVIOLET RAYS

OZONE LAYER

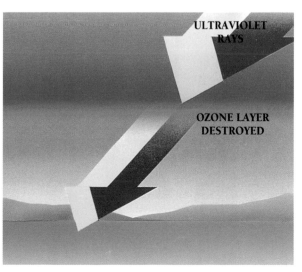

ULTRAVIOLET RAYS

OZONE LAYER DESTROYED

HOT AND COLD

The hotness or coldness of the air (air temperature), the amount of moisture in the air (air humidity), and the weight of the air (air pressure) are the elements in the atmosphere that create weather. The element that people are most aware of is temperature.

Temperature varies according to time of day and time of year. It is colder in winter, when the earth tilts us away from the sun, and at night, when our side of the earth faces away from the sun.

A thermometer is used to measure temperature. The most common type of thermometer consists of a glass tube that contains mercury or alcohol. When these liquids become warm, their volume increases and they move up the tube. When the temperature decreases, the liquid moves down the tube. A scale on the outside of the tube allows the change in temperature to be measured precisely.

The U-shaped maximum and minimum thermometer uses mercury and alcohol. The figures opposite the lower ends of the tiny metal markers in the two columns record the highest and lowest temperatures, respectively.

Weather is a combination of three elements in the atmosphere: temperature, humidity, and pressure.

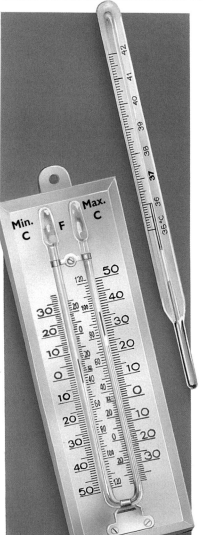

Temperature is measured in specific units. On the Fahrenheit scale, water freezes at 32°F and boils at 212°F. On the Celsius scale, water freezes at 0°C, and boils at 100°C. Scientists use the Kelvin scale, on which water freezes at 273 K and boils at 373 K.

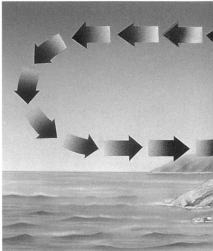

The average temperature of any place in the world depends on the amount of the sun's heat it receives. As the map of temperature zones shows, the closer an area is to the equator, the hotter it is likely to be. The lowest temperatures are found at the poles.

	Cold all year
	Warm summer Cold winter
	Hot summer Cold winter
	Cool summer Mild winter
	Hot summer Mild winter
	Hot all year

COLD AIR

WARM AIR

Other factors complicate this simple picture. Seawater warms up and cools down more quickly than does land. On a sunny day, the land warms rapidly. The air above gets lighter and rises, and a cool breeze from the sea moves in to replace it. At night, the opposite happens. Cooler land air replaces warmer air over the sea. As a result, coastal areas tend to have steady temperatures.

Height also affects temperature. The temperature of dry air falls by 1.8°F (1°C) for every 328 feet (100 m) of height. Mountainous areas are, therefore, normally cooler than lowland areas. A mountain, however, can cause the land at its base to be cooler. On a clear, calm night, cool mountain air may sink downhill to replace the warmer air below, which creates a cold downhill wind.

The normal temperature of a place depends not only on its nearness to the equator but also its altitude and proximity to the sea.

AIR PRESSURE

Although it feels weightless, air has weight. Its weight is not noticeable because the pressure of the air in our bodies is the same as that of the air around us. Air, or atmospheric, pressure changes from place to place and from time to time. Heat makes air less dense, so warm air is lighter than cold air. Because it is lighter, warm air rises, while heavier cold air sinks and flows to take its place.

If the earth were still and did not spin, the hot air at the equator would rise and go directly to the poles, while cold air from the poles would flow straight to the equator to replace it. But the spin deflects the flow of air to form spirals. In the northern hemisphere, these spirals flow from left to right in areas of high pressure and from right to left in areas of low pressure. They flow in the opposite directions south of the equator.

Warm rising air causes low pressure, while cold descending air causes high pressure. Winds, which are air on the move, naturally blow from high pressure to low pressure. Hot air at the equator rises and creates areas of low pressure. As the rising air cools, it spreads out to the north and south, where it sinks and becomes warmer, which causes areas of high pressure. The warm air flows toward the equator, and the whole cycle begins again.

Weather maps use isobars to show air pressure. Isobars are lines that link places where the pressure is the same, in the way that contour lines on ordinary maps join places of the same height. Air pressure is measured in millibars. Average pressure at sea level is 1,013 millibars. Circles at the center of isobar systems

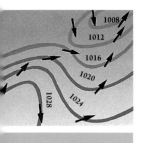

On weather maps, air pressure is shown by isobars. The higher the figure is in millibars, the higher the pressure.

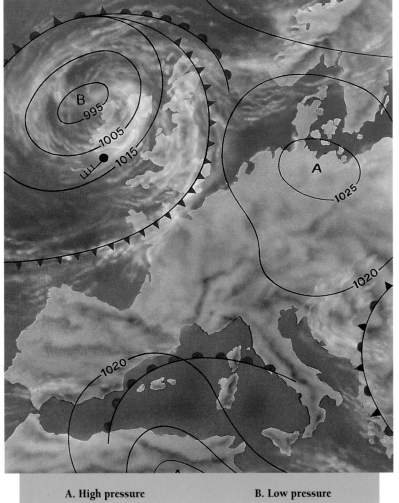

A. High pressure   B. Low pressure

indicate areas of high and low pressure.

Air pressure is measured with a barometer. The Italian scientist Torricelli invented this simple instrument by chance in 1643, during his experiments to create a vacuum. Torricelli filled a thin tube with mercury, turned it upside down, and plunged it into a bowl of mercury. As soon as the tube was in position, the column of mercury sank down inside the tube until it remained steady at a height of about 29.6 inches (76 cm). Above the mercury, in the empty part of the tube, Torricelli found the vacuum he had sought. It soon became obvious that the mercury level changed with the weather and that it rose or fell according to height above sea level. This led to the discovery of air pressure, which is higher at sea level than in the mountains.

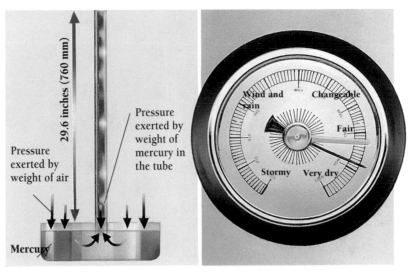

Mercury barometers have largely been replaced by aneroid barometers. These instruments are based on a flexible metal box that contains a partial vacuum. Changes in air pressure squeeze or relax a box that is linked to a pointer. The pointer moves around a dial that is graduated in millibars and marked with the expected weather conditions.

The words on the dial of a barometer—stormy, wind and rain, changeable, fair and very dry—give an idea of the weather to be expected.

WHAT A WIND!

1. Prevailing westerlies
2. Northeast trade winds
3. Equatorial doldrums
4. Hurricanes
5. Southeast trade winds
6. Prevailing westerlies
7. Southern polar winds
8. Typhoons
9. Cyclones

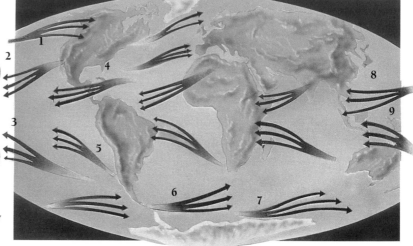

In spite of many local variations, there is a general pattern of air circulation around the world. It takes the form of broad bands that circle the earth parallel to the equator. Apart from the almost windless zone on the equator, each of these bands is dominated by a prevailing wind. Although these winds are not constant, they blow more often than any other wind in the same area.

Rising air at the equator causes calm conditions known as the doldrums. Immediately to the north is a zone where steady northeast winds blow. These are called the trade winds, because merchant ships that had sails took advantage of them. Farther north is a band of prevailing westerlies. Beyond it are bitter polar winds that blow from the east. This wind pattern is true of the northern hemisphere. The pattern in the south is the same. Some violent winds blow only for a short time, but they bring dreadful devastation. Areas both north and south of the equator experience particularly violent winds at certain times of the year. Called typhoons or cyclones in the Pacific and hurricanes in the Caribbean, they are whirlpools of air up to 372 miles (600 km) across that blow at very high speeds. They form over warm sea but die away over land.

Winds are caused by differences in temperature and air pressure. Their direction is affected by the earth's rotation and by local conditions.

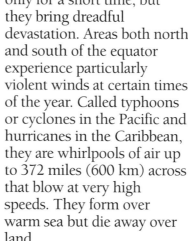

Some local winds blow so regularly that they are given names. The sirocco is a southeast wind that carries desert dust from the Sahara to parts of Europe. The same name is given to a warm damp wind that blows from the same direction but brings rain. The harmattan is a cool wind that blows southward from northwest Africa. It is so dry that it withers vegetation and may cause people's skin to peel.

Wind speed is measured with a simple instrument called an anemometer. It consists of cups mounted on arms that rotate around a central spindle. The wind fills the cups and makes them turn. The stronger the wind, the faster the cups rotate. The number of turns the cups make in a second is shown on a dial by a pointer coupled to the spindle. It gives the wind speed in meters per second.

A weather vane or a wind

from and its strength.

In 1805, the British admiral Francis Beaufort devised a scale to estimate wind speeds. A variation on the scale is shown above: 1. Light air: smoke drifts with air. 2. Light breeze: smoke is blown and leaves rustle. 3. Gentle breeze: leaves and twigs move. 4. Moderate breeze: small branches in constant motion. 5. Fresh breeze: small trees sway, and waves form on inland waters. 6. Strong

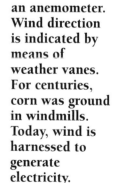

Wind speeds are measured with an anemometer. Wind direction is indicated by means of weather vanes. For centuries, corn was ground in windmills. Today, wind is harnessed to generate electricity.

sock shows wind direction. A weathercock is the traditional kind of weather vane. The bird's beak points to where the wind comes from. The wind sock is a more reliable device. It is a tube made of sturdy cloth that is open at both ends. One end is tethered to a rigid ring. When the wind blows, the sock rises and trails in the wind. It shows at a glance the direction the wind comes

breeze: large branches sway and electric cables whistle. 7. Near gale: trees bend and it is difficult to walk into the wind. 8. Gale: twigs break and it is very difficult to walk. 9. Strong gale: tiles ripped from roofs. 10. Storm: trees uprooted, buildings damaged. 11. Violent storm: widespread severe damage. 12. Hurricane: devastation. When it is dead calm, the wind force is 0.

WATER IN THE AIR

Water vapor is a gas that you cannot see, feel, or smell. Humidity is the amount of water vapor in the air. Air is saturated when it cannot hold any more water vapor. Warm air can hold more water vapor than cold air, so when warm, moist air cools down, the air eventually becomes saturated. As the air becomes saturated, the water vapor it holds condenses to form tiny water droplets that appear as mist or fog. Fog (A) is defined as any condensation that reduces visibility to less than half a mile. Mist (B) is a haze that reduces visibility only slightly.

You can make your own fog if you breathe on a window on a cold day. Your breath, which is saturated air, cools when it hits the cold glass and turns into water droplets.

Relative humidity is the amount of water vapor in the air compared with the amount required for saturation at the same temperature. It can be measured with a hair hygrometer. This instrument uses human hair, which is at its shortest when dry and gradually grows longer as it gets wet. A bundle of hair is anchored at one end and attached to a lever at the other. As the hair length changes, the lever moves a pointer on a scale.

Air contains water in the form of an invisible gas called water vapor. As air cools, the water vapor turns into water droplets that become visible as fog or mist.

A

B

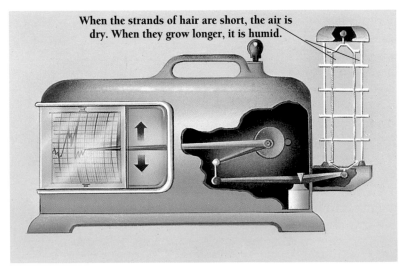

When the strands of hair are short, the air is dry. When they grow longer, it is humid.

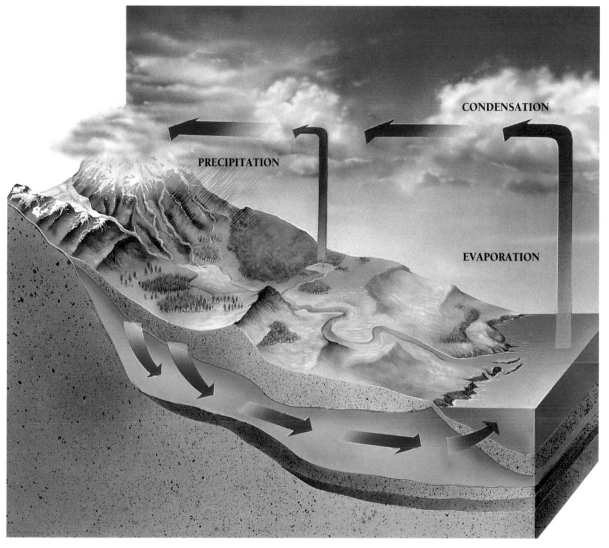

CONDENSATION

PRECIPITATION

EVAPORATION

Water moves in an unending process like a turning wheel. As water vapor, it rises into the sky where it turns into water droplets and forms clouds. The water droplets join together to make larger drops that fall to earth as rain.

The sun's rays heat the surface of the oceans, seas, and lakes. The heat makes the water evaporate and turn into water vapor. As the air is warmed by the sun's heat, it becomes lighter, and some sweeps toward the land. When the moisture-laden winds meet the land, they are forced to rise, often by high mountains. As the air rises, it cools. The water vapor in the colder air condenses to form minute water droplets. The tiny droplets formed in rising air join together in larger drops that collect to become clouds.

The drops become too heavy to float in the air, so they fall back to earth as rain, or if it is cold enough, as snow or hail. Rain, snow, and hail are grouped together under the term precipitation. Almost all of the water that evaporates from the oceans falls back into them. The rest mostly falls on the land, soaks into the soil, and seeps into the rocks. This water finds its way back to a river and is carried to the sea.

Once the water has returned to the sea, the processes of evaporation, rising, cooling, condensation, and rainfall are repeated and go on indefinitely. This never-ending process is called the water cycle.

CLOUDS

A cloud is a great mass of billions of tiny water droplets or ice crystals. When air rises and is cooled enough to reach its saturation point, the water vapor in it condenses. A boiling kettle illustrates this process: The water vapor at the spout is cooled by the air it meets. It condenses and forms steam—a small cloud.

Clouds are formed when air is cooled below its saturation point. When air passes over a warm land surface, it heats up and rises. As it rises, it cools and forms clouds. Air must rise when it blows over mountains, and this makes it form clouds. Lighter warm air rides up over heavier cold air.

Clouds often change their shape when they evaporate or condense. Some are white and fluffy, others dark and menacing. Their names describe their appearance. Cirrus clouds are wispy (cirro means "curl"), cumulus clouds are like heaps of cotton wool (cumulo means "heap"), and stratus clouds are sheets that often cover the whole sky (stratus means "layer"). Different clouds form at different heights in the sky. The main cloud names are used in various combinations to describe their appearance and height.

When warm air rises and cools down, the water vapor it holds condenses as water droplets to form clouds.

CIRROSTRATUS clouds are thin sheets of ice crystals that look like a veil. They occur at heights of 22,966 feet (7,000 m) and above.

ALTOSTRATUS clouds consist of water droplets. They form a smooth gray sheet of cloud at about 9,843 feet (3,000 m). Altostratus causes drizzle rather than rain.

STRATUS is the lowest kind of cloud. It forms a low, gray sheet with a base that ranges from ground level to about 984 feet (300 m). At ground level, stratus clouds form fog.

NIMBOSTRATUS is a sheet of gray cloud that produces continuous rain or snow. Its base varies between 1,969 feet (600 m) and 8,202 feet (2,500 m) and may be thick enough to reach 19,685 feet (6,000 m).

CIRROCUMULUS is caused by strong winds at very high altitudes. It usually appears in small patches that may look like fish scales. This kind of cirrocumulus is known as a mackerel sky.

CIRRUS clouds look like wispy streaks of white hair, sometimes called mares' tails. They are composed of ice crystals and found as high as 32,808 feet (10,000 m).

CUMULONIMBUS are towering anvil-shaped thunderclouds that pile up high in the sky and discharge rain, hail, and lightning. They may be 6.2 miles (10 km) across and 6.2 miles (10 km) high.

ALTOCUMULUS is found between 8,202 feet (2,500 m) and 19,685 feet (6,000 m). Made of water droplets, it appears as layers of puffy white or gray clouds that signal a change in the weather.

CUMULUS are white puffy clouds that often float in the sky on sunny days. Sometimes, they join together and produce rain or cumulonimbus clouds.

STRATOCUMULUS clouds form in pale or dark layers and often extend over thousands of square miles. They create an overcast sky but rarely give rain.

Get to know the ever-changing cloud types and you will always know what kind of weather to expect.

RAIN, SNOW AND HAIL

The water particles in a cloud are so tiny that it takes millions of them to form one raindrop. They grow bigger when they collide with each other or when more moisture condenses on them. Eventually, they become heavy enough to fall as raindrops. Raindrops measure between .078 inch (2 mm) and .195 inch (5 mm) in diameter. Larger drops splash when they hit the ground. The smallest drops land lightly as drizzle.

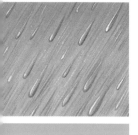

Rain is vital to life. In parts of the world where rain is scarce, there are few plants, animals, or people.

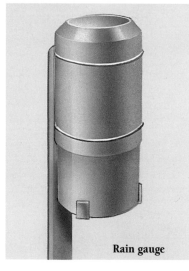

Rain gauge

Rainfall is measured with a rain gauge. This instrument is a cylinder with a removable lid. Inside is a funnel that leads to a tube. The mouth of the funnel is ten times the diameter of the tube, so if one inch of rain falls, it will measure ten inches on the tube. This makes it possible to measure very small amounts of rain. The gauge should be placed on the ground in the open.

When air cools, some of the water vapor in it condenses. On a clear, cold night, the ground loses heat quickly. If the air above it is cooled sufficiently, it becomes saturated and condenses as droplets of dew on plants and on the ground. The air temperature at which dew begins to form is called the dew point. When the temperature is below freezing, ice crystals are deposited as frost.

When the temperature in a cloud falls to below 14°F (-10°C), water vapor turns into ice crystals. The upper parts of many clouds consist of ice crystals. If these grow too heavy, they fall through the cloud and collide with water droplets that freeze on them. The crystals join together to form snowflakes. A typical snowflake may consist of 50 or more individual ice crystals. As the snow crystals pass through warmer air, they may melt and fall as rain. But if the temperature is cold enough, they fall as snow. Sometimes snow and rain fall together as sleet.

If you look at a snow crystal under a magnifying glass, you will see that it has six sides or points. Look at another crystal and you will see the same, but the pattern will be different. Every individual snowflake has its own shape. No two are ever exactly the same.

Snow takes up more space than rain composed of the same amount of water. As a rough guide, 1.9 inches (5 cm) of rain equals 19.5 inches (50 cm) of fallen snow.

Water also falls as hail. Hailstones are made of layers of ice. They form in high cumulus clouds. Droplets of water are tossed up and down the freezing levels of the cloud by air currents. Water condenses on them as they fall and freezes as they rise. Eventually, they fall to earth as hail. Some hailstones are as big as tennis balls. A large hailstone that is cut open will show many layers of ice.

AIR MASSES AND FRONTS

Air masses are enormous bodies of air that form over areas of land or sea with a fairly constant temperature. They may be warm or cold, humid or dry. Air masses move at different speeds and do not easily mix. The boundary zones between them are called fronts. Most changes in the weather occur along fronts. There are two main types of front: cold and warm.

In a cold front, when cold air catches up with warmer air, it burrows underneath the warmer air, which causes it to rise rapidly and cool down. As it cools, the water vapor in the warm air condenses and falls as heavy rain. As the front passes, it brings colder weather.

A warm front occurs when warm air overtakes cooler air. The warm air rides up gradually over the colder air, which causes the water vapor it holds to fall as gentle rain or drizzle. As the front passes, it brings warmer weather.

Cold air moves faster than warm air, so a cold front often catches up with a warm front to form an occluded front. An occluded front generally results in persistent clouds and rain.

Air masses blow from one area to another. The boundaries between air masses of different temperatures and humidity levels are known as fronts.

On weather maps, cold fronts are indicated on their leading edge by triangles, warm fronts by semicircles, and occluded fronts by alternating triangles and semicircles.

■ Cold air masses	■ Warm air masses	

Cold front

Warm front

Occluded front

| WARM FRONT | Cirrus | Altocumulus | Numbostratus |

Cirrus clouds are the first indication of the arrival of a warm front. Then the sky begins to cloud over. Altocumulus clouds appear and the wind picks up. The clouds thicken to altostratus and soon turn to a low, dark blanket of nimbostratus. It starts to rain or snow steadily for hours at a time. A warm front advances slowly at about 4.9 miles per hour (8 km/h). The clouds that are the first signs of its approach may be seen 930 miles (1,500 km) in advance of the front at ground level and 48 hours before the front's arrival.

Cold fronts often follow warm fronts. They move at about 18.6 miles per hour (30 km/h), considerably faster than warm fronts. The front's arrival is signaled by strong gusts of wind, large clouds, and bursts of heavy rain, hail, or even thunderstorms. When the storm passes and the clouds clear, it is cooler. Some cumulus clouds may remain to cause further downpours.

Warm fronts and cold fronts both bring rain. Warm front rain tends to be persistent and moderate. Rain from cold fronts is usually violent but short-lived.

| COLD FRONT | Wind | Rain or hail | Cumulus |

STORMY WEATHER

Hurricanes and typhoons are the largest and most powerful of storms. Tornadoes are smaller but more violent.

Tropical storms can be predicted, but they still bring devastation and death. Known as hurricanes in the Atlantic and typhoons in the Pacific, cyclones are huge whirling storms that are born in hot, moist air masses over the oceans slightly north or south of the equator. There, in late summer and early autumn, trade winds from the northern hemisphere meet trade winds from the south. The twisting effect of the earth's rotation makes them whirl around each other.

Cyclones feed on the energy they get from warm moist air when they move over the ocean. Their winds grow increasingly violent and reach speeds of 149 miles per hour (240 km/h) that can rise to 224 miles per hour (360 km/h) in sudden gusts. At the center, or eye, of the cyclone is an area of calm about 6.8 miles (11 km) across. Cyclones wreak enormous havoc in coastal areas but die down as they move inland.

Tornadoes are small cyclones. They occur on land during spring and summer in places where moist warm air and cold air masses meet. They consist of funnels of wind that whirl at speeds of up to 280 miles per hour (450 km/h) or more around a center in which air pressure is so low that it sometimes causes buildings to explode. Tornadoes are short-lived and rarely measure more than 4,921 feet (1,500 m) across. The most violent tornadoes occur in the United States.

Thunderstorms occur when warm, moist air is forced upward by air currents or by a mass of cold air that burrows under a mass of warm air. They are set in motion by updrafts of air, usually in large cumulonimbus clouds. These winds cause water drops and ice crystals in the cloud to rub together, which builds up gigantic charges of static electricity. Cloud particles become alternately positively and negatively charged. When enough electricity has been produced, it is released as a lightning flash between two clouds or between a cloud and the ground. Thunder is the sound made by air in the path of the flash, which expands violently when it is heated by the electricity in the flash. Violent thunderstorms occur almost daily in equatorial regions. They occur least often in the polar regions, which lack the heat that generates thunderstorms.

Because light travels much faster than sound, you always see lightning before you hear the thunder it causes.

Rainbows occur when sunlight is seen through raindrops. The raindrops break up the sun's white light and reflect it back to an observer as seven different colors—red, orange, yellow, green, blue, indigo, and violet—the colors of the rainbow. You can only see a rainbow when you stand with your back to the sun. Large raindrops produce the best rainbows. Sometimes, you may be lucky enough to see a double rainbow.

WEATHER FORECASTING

Long ago, people looked for clues in nature to help them predict the weather. The sound of frogs croaking loudly was a sign of rain on the way. Closed pinecones meant wet weather; open ones meant sunny weather. The rhyme, "Red sky at night, sailors delight. Red sky in the morning, sailors take warning," is probably the best-known example of traditional weather wisdom. Watch the sky and see if it is true.

Satellites and sophisticated modern computers have revolutionized weather forecasting. Satellites in stationary or variable orbits provide pictures of weather worldwide. Radar provides details of cloud cover and rainfall. Further contributions come from weather ships, weather observatories, and balloon-borne equipment. This diverse information is digested and processed by weather-forecasting computers that are capable of making billions of calculations per second. Meteorologists translate the computer results into weather forecasts for aircraft, ships, and farmers; into reports for radio and television; into maps for newspapers; and into temperature forecasts for the gas and electricity industries.

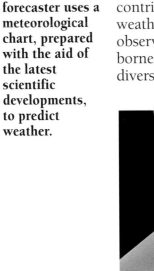

A weather forecaster uses a meteorological chart, prepared with the aid of the latest scientific developments, to predict weather.

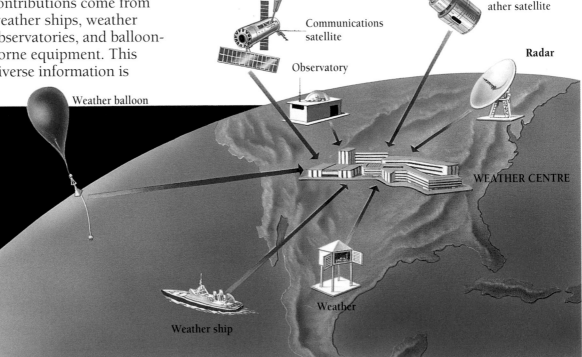

Communications satellite

Geostationary weather satellite

Observatory

Radar

Weather balloon

WEATHER CENTRE

Weather ship

Weather

There are basically three types of climate: hot, temperate, and cold. Temperatures go from hot at the equator to cold at the poles. Temperature is affected not only by latitude but also by altitude, ocean currents, and distance from the sea. Rainfall also varies from place to place because of the prevailing winds and the rise and fall of the land.

TROPICAL CLIMATE

DESERT CLIMATE

MEDITERRANEAN CLIMATE

CONTINENTAL CLIMATE

The frozen wastes of the Arctic and Antarctic are dry and extremely cold. The same climate occurs in mountainous regions that have snow and ice all year. These areas are as hostile to life as hot deserts, and little grows in them. Because temperate regions are neither too hot nor too cold, neither too wet nor too dry, they are good for growing crops and grazing animals.

The frozen wilderness of polar regions and the damp heat of equatorial forests represent the opposite extremes of world climates.

Equatorial climates are hot and humid all year. Tropical climates have humid summers and dry winters. Rain forests thrive in these regions, but the soil is poor and it is hard to grow crops. Oceanic regions mostly have mild summers and winters. The Mediterranean climate gives hot, dry summers and gentle, damp winters. The continental climate inland has hot summers and cold winters.

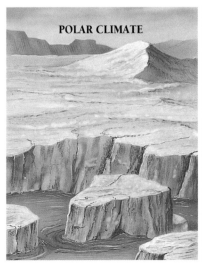

POLAR CLIMATE

MOUNTAIN CLIMATE

FUTURE WEATHER

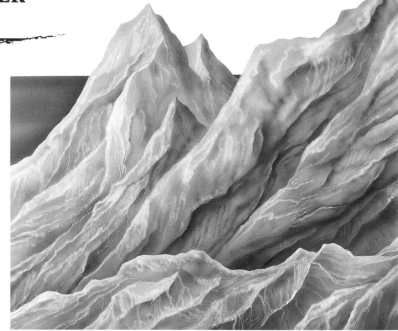

In the past, the earth's climate has changed many times. From 80,000 to 10,000 years ago, most of northern Europe, Asia, and North America was covered in ice, in places 1.2 miles (2 km) thick. This ice age was only the most recent of many, and scientists are still not sure what caused it or its predecessors. Although humans are now living in a warmer phase, it seems that the global climate is ready to change again.

Whatever may have caused previous ice ages, past climatic changes have arisen from natural causes. The change to a warmer global climate that many scientists now predict is due not to natural forces but to human activity. Attempts are being made to halt the change, but it may be too late.

Carbon dioxide and other gases that occur naturally in the atmosphere help to keep the earth warm enough to sustain life. These gases let the sun's rays through to heat the earth but prevent too much heat from being radiated back into space. They are called greenhouse gases because they act like the glass in a greenhouse. When heat passes through the glass into the greenhouse, the surfaces and plants inside get hot and heat the air. The heat gradually passes out through the glass but only very slowly.

Too much carbon dioxide in the atmosphere, however, increases the greenhouse

Pollution is changing the balance of gases in the atmosphere, which causes global warming.

GREENHOUSE EFFECT

1. Heat from the sun

2. Natural gases

3. Pollution gases

4. Radiation trapped

5. Heat escaping into space

effect, so that extra heat is trapped. During the last fifty years, cars and factories have poured huge and ever-increasing volumes of carbon dioxide and other pollutants into the atmosphere. It is impossible to predict accurately what will happen as a result. It is possible that polar ice caps may melt and rising seas may flood low-lying coastal areas.

Smoke from factories and

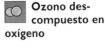

Ozono descompuesto en oxígeno

Cloro procedente de los CFC, clorofluo-ro-carbonos compuestos, usados en espráis y refrigeradores, que destruyen las moléculas de oxígeno

car exhausts combines with natural fog to create a lethal mixture known as smog. Smoke particles and sulfuric acid in smog can be fatal to anyone with breathing difficulties. In some big cities, the combination of pollutants and hot sunshine produces a photochemical smog that blocks out the sun and causes a temperature inversion. What would otherwise be a warm, sunny day becomes cool and gloomy.

The ozone layer shields the earth from overexposure to ultraviolet radiation that can cause skin cancer and eye diseases. Widespread use of CFCs has caused large holes to open up in the ozone layer over the poles. The use of these chemicals has now been limited but not yet totally banned. Although ozone high in the atmosphere protects us, at ground level it is a pollutant, a component of photochemical smog.

The earth's forests are shrinking fast, as they are cut down for their wood or cleared for cultivation or industrial developments. This also changes the world's climate, because trees absorb carbon dioxide and give off water vapor. A square mile of tropical forest evaporates more moisture than the same area of ocean. More carbon dioxide increases global warming, and less water vapor means less rain.

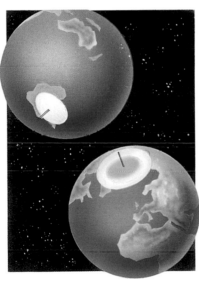

Trees are also damaged by acid rain. Emissions of sulfur and nitrogen compounds by factories, power stations, and cars combine with water vapor to form acids. These acids fall to the ground by themselves or in rain. When they collect in rivers and lakes, the acids weaken and kill fish and other wildlife. Clouds blown from industrial areas may dump their lethal rain on forests far away, which causes the trees to die.

Pollution shrouds cities in smog or subjects them to showers of acid rain. On a piece of graph paper, make a chart of the daily rainfall totals from your rain gauge.

Wind

Water vapor

Oxides of sulfur and nitrogen

Rain

Dust

Acid droplets

WORKING WITH WEATHER

Meteorology is the science of weather. Meteorologists not only watch the weather and forecast future weather, but also study why the weather is the way it is and what causes it. Like other scientists, they test their theories. With the aid of simple, everyday objects, it is possible to prove at home some of the processes that cause weather.

WHICH HEATS FASTER?
Take two plastic glasses and fill one with dry soil from a shady place and the other with cool water. Put both glasses out in the hot sun. After an hour, take their temperatures with a thermometer. Then move both glasses into the shade for an hour and do the same. Which substance warms more quickly and which cools more quickly?

MAKE A RAIN GAUGE
Ask an adult to cut off the top of a plastic bottle. Place the top upside down in the bottom part and attach it with adhesive tape. Place a paper strip marked in half inches on the side of the bottle, and fill the bottle to where your scale starts. Put your rain gauge in a flowerpot and leave it out in the open. Now take daily readings of the rainfall.

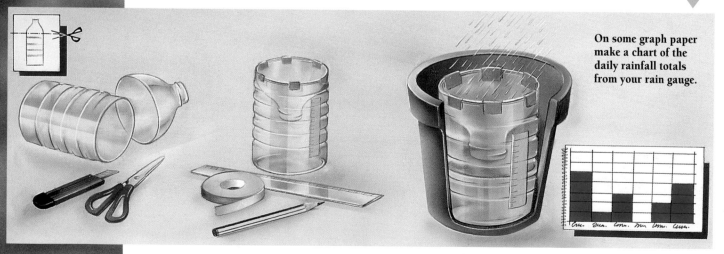

On some graph paper make a chart of the daily rainfall totals from your rain gauge.

TESTING FOR ACID RAIN

First, make an indicator. Ask an adult to boil some chopped red cabbage in a small amount of distilled water for a few minutes, then let it stand for an hour. Strain the cabbage and keep the cabbage water. Do not let it drain down the sink. Pour equal amounts of the purple cabbage water into a glass of distilled water and a glass of rainwater. If the rainwater turns red, you have acid rain in your area.

MAKE YOUR OWN RAINBOW

You will need a clear glass of water and a sheet of white paper for this experiment. Lay the paper on a window ledge and place the glass on it in full sunlight. What can you see on the paper in the shade of the glass? If you do not see a rainbow, put a piece of card between the glass and the window with a narrow slit in it so that only a sliver of sunlight can get through.

MAKE A WEATHER RECORD

Draw up a weather chart like this one for each month. Watch the sky every day and record what you see. Every day look at your rain gauge and at a thermometer and enter the results on your weather chart.

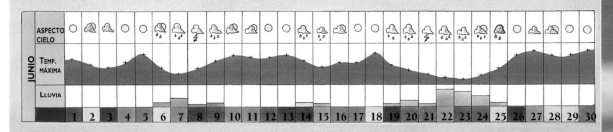

GLOSSARY

ACID RAIN Rain that contains high levels of acids derived from pollution.

AIR Mixture of gases—including nitrogen, oxygen, and carbon dioxide—that make up the atmosphere.

AIR MASS Large body of air in which the temperature, humidity, and pressure are nearly consistent.

AIR PRESSURE Weight of air. Also called atmospheric pressure.

ALTITUDE Another word for height. anemometer Instrument that measures wind speed.

ANEROID BAROMETER See barometer.

ATMOSPHERE Blanket of air that surrounds and protects the earth.

ATMOSPHERIC PRESSURE See air pressure.

ATOM Tiny particle of matter, once thought to be indivisible.

AURORA Sheet of colored light that is sometimes seen in the night sky at the poles.

BAROMETER Instrument for measuring air pressure.

BEAUFORT SCALE Scale of numbers used to indicate the wind's strength.

CLOUD Mass of condensed water vapor that floats in the air.

CONDENSATION Process in which a gas turns into a liquid, as when water vapor turns into rain.

CYCLONE Winds that spiral around a center of low pressure. Hurricanes, typhoons, and tornadoes are cyclones.

DEW Moisture deposited overnight by cool air that condenses on plants and other cold surfaces.

DOLDRUMS Area of calm weather and low pressure near the equator where the northeast and southeast trade winds meet.

EQUATOR Imaginary line that runs east-west around the middle of the earth.

EVAPORATION Process in which a liquid turns into a gas. The opposite of condensation.

FOG Cloud at ground level that restricts visibility.

FRONT Boundary between two different air masses. A cold front is one where colder air begins to overtake warmer air. A warm front is one where warmer air catches up with colder air. An occluded front occurs when a cold front overtakes a warm front.

FROST Frozen dew.

GLOBAL WARMING Increase in temperatures worldwide that some scientists believe began to occur as a result of increased carbon dioxide emissions.

GREENHOUSE EFFECT Ability of atmospheric gases to hold a layer of warm air near the earth's surface. Too much carbon dioxide increases the effect and traps extra heat.

HAIL Pellets of frozen rain formed from layers of ice.

HARMATTAN Dry local wind in West Africa.

HEMISPHERE Half of a sphere. The earth is divided into eastern and western hemispheres and northern and southern hemispheres.

HUMIDITY The amount of water vapor in the air.

HURRICANE Violent cyclone that forms in the Caribbean or eastern Pacific.

ICE AGE Period of several thousand years in which large parts of the earth were covered in thick ice sheets.

INFRARED RADIATION Rays from the sun that heat the earth.

ISOBAR Line on a weather map that joins points of equal air pressure.

MERCURY Liquid metal used in thermometers and barometers.

METEOROLOGY Study of the atmosphere and particularly weather. millibar Unit of air pressure, one-thousandth of a bar.

MIST Thin cloud at ground level. molecule Unit of matter composed of atoms.

OCCLUDED FRONT See front.

OZONE Form of oxygen that forms a layer in the stratosphere and absorbs harmful ultraviolet radiation from the sun.

CHLOROFLUOROCARBONS (CFCS) Chemical compounds used in refrigerants, aerosols, and other products that rise as gases into the atmosphere and damage the ozone layer.

POLES Points, north and south, that mark the ends of the earth's axis. precipitation Rain, snow, or hail that falls from a cloud.

PREVAILING WIND Wind that blows most often from one direction.

RADIATION Rays of light and heat, and other rays from the sun.

SATURATED Full of moisture. When the air is saturated, the water condenses to form dew.

SHOOTING STAR Bright, moving trail of light seen in the night sky when a meteor (matter from outer space) burns up in the atmosphere.

SIROCCO 1. Dry wind that reaches Europe from the Sahara. 2. Warm rainy wind that blows in southern Europe.

SMOG Mixture of smoke and fog. temperate Moderate climate with four seasons.

TEMPERATURE Degree of heat.

THERMOMETER Instrument used to measure temperature.

TORNADO Violent whirlwind.

TRADE WIND Wind that blows steadily toward the equator. North of the equator, trade winds come from the northeast; south of it, they come from the southeast.

TYPHOON Name used for a hurricane that arises in the western Pacific.

ULTRAVIOLET (UV) Rays in sunlight that can tan and damage the skin.

WATER VAPOR Water in the form of an invisible gas in the atmosphere.

WEATHER State of the atmosphere in a particular place at a particular time. It includes temperature, pressure, humidity, wind, and cloudiness.

WEATHERCOCK Traditional instrument that indicates wind strength and direction.

WIND Moving air.

WIND SOCK Device that indicates wind strength and direction.

INDEX